PICTURE WINDOW BOOKS
a capstone imprint

Editor: Julie Gassman
Designer: Ashlee Suker
Art Director: Nathan Gassman
Production Specialist: Laura Manthe
The illustrations in this book were created with watercolor.

Picture Window Books
1710 Roe Crest Drive
North Mankato, MN 56003
www.capstonepub.com

Library of Congress Cataloging-in-Publication Data
Manushkin, Fran.
What's in your heart, Katie?: writing in a journal with Katie Woo / by Fran Manushkin ; illustrated by Tammie Lyon.
p. cm. — (Katie Woo, star writer)
Includes sidebars about keeping a journal and the kinds of things you can write in one.
Summary: When Katie misplaces her lucky charm, her mother gives her a journal to write her feelings in.
ISBN 978-1-4048-8127-3 (library binding)
ISBN 978-1-4795-1922-4 (paperback)
ISBN 978-1-4795-1888-3 (ebook pdf)
1. Woo, Katie (Fictitious character)—Juvenile fiction. 2. Chinese Americans—Juvenile fiction. 3. Diaries—Juvenile fiction. [1. Chinese Americans—Fiction. 2. Diaries—Fiction.] I. Lyon, Tammie, ill. II. Title. III. Title: What is in your heart, Katie?

PZ7.M3195Whg 2013
813.54—dc23 2013004208

Printed in the United States of America in Stevens Point, Wisconsin.
032013 007227WZF13

What's in Your Heart, Katie?

Writing in a Journal with Katie Woo

by Fran Manushkin

illustrated by Tammie Lyon

Katie lost her lucky charm. "I can't find it anywhere," she groaned. "Now I won't have good luck!"

"Don't worry," said her mom. "I'm sure you will have good luck."

She gave Katie a pretty notebook.

"When I was your age, I had a journal," she said. "Writing in it made me feel better."

"I'll try it," said Katie.

She wrote:

I lost my lucky charm! I'm very worried. I hope this journal brings me good luck!

Katie's Star Tip

My journal is a notebook. Some people use fancy books with blank pages. Some people use plain paper. Guess what? You can type your journal on a computer. Choose the kind of journal that's the best for you!

Katie asked her mom, "What else can I write?"

"Write about what happens to you," said her mom.

"But what if nothing happens?" asked Katie.

Her mother smiled. "Don't worry," she said. "Something always does."

Katie's Star Tip

You can fill your journal with surprising and odd things that you notice. For example, my dad sneezes so loud, it makes me jump! I loved writing that down.

Katie went outside. It was a lovely day. The sun was hot, but the breeze felt cool.

Katie wrote:

How funny! I feel cold and warm at the same time!

"I can't wait to show JoJo my journal," said Katie. But JoJo wasn't home.

"Now I'm feeling unlucky," Katie sighed. She wrote in her journal:

A day without JoJo
is a very sad day.

Katie's Star Tip

A journal is a wonderful place to write down your feelings: happy feelings, sad feelings, angry feelings. All feelings have a home in your journal!

Katie hurried to Pedro's house.

"Do you have a journal?" Katie asked him.

"I don't," said Pedro. "But I have a new soccer ball. Let's kick it around."

Katie and Pedro played soccer.

They both scored goals!

Katie wrote in her journal:

Today I played soccer with Pedro.
Running and kicking makes me
feel strong. I love that!

Katie's Star Tip

Writing in your journal helps you remember important things. Weeks and months can go by, but your memories will always be there—safe in your journal!

Katie played with Pedro's baby brother too.

"He smells so sweet," said Katie.

"Not all the time," said Pedro's mom.

Katie wrote in her journal:

Sometimes Pedro's brother
is stinky!

She read it to Pedro, and he laughed.

"I'll tell you a secret," he whispered.

"What is it?" asked Katie.

“When my brother cries a lot, I go outside where it’s nice and quiet,” said Pedro. “It makes me feel better.”

“Good for you,” said Katie. “Why don’t you write that in a journal?”

“I will!” decided Pedro.

"I wonder what will happen to me next?" said Katie. "I hope it is something lucky."

It was! A butterfly landed on Katie's hand.

"Oh, my," Katie whispered to the butterfly. "You are so light! I wish I could fly like you or like a seagull. I'll write that in my journal. It's a good place to put wishes."

Katie's Star Tip

Everyone has wishes and dreams—big ones and little ones. Writing about them adds to the fun. You can also use your journal to set goals for yourself. One of my goals is to do 10 cartwheels in a row. My wish is that I find my good luck charm. I really miss it!

Katie went back to JoJo's house.

JoJo was home!

"JoJo, I have a journal!" said Katie.
"I'm writing about what I see and feel
and do."

"I have a journal too," said JoJo. "I keep my secrets in it."

"What are your secrets?" asked Katie eagerly.

"I can't tell you." JoJo laughed. "They are secrets!"

Katie's Star Tip

A journal is the perfect place for your secrets. My secret is: Grandma gave me a new green sweater, but I'm not wild about it. I won't tell Grandma, but I can tell my journal.

JoJo and Katie shared a big piece of pie. Suddenly JoJo said, “Okay, I’ll tell you a secret. My middle name is Dolores.”

“I like that name!” said Katie.

JoJo smiled. “I’m so glad!”

Katie and JoJo wrote in their journals. Katie wrote:

I have a bff! Guess who?
JoJo!

JoJo wrote:

May 5,
I like Katie so much,
I told her my secret!

Katie's Star Tip

JoJo put the date at the top of her journal entry. When you do that, you will remember the exact day something happened.

On the way home, Katie wrote in her journal:

It's fun to share secrets with friends. My birthday is next week, but I've told everybody, so that's not a secret.

Writing in a journal is fun! I wonder if Mom and Dad have secrets. I can't wait to ask them.

Katie's Star Tip

Do you know the best thing about writing in a journal? YOU make the rules! You can be serious. You can be silly. You don't have to worry about complete sentences either. Get out your crayons and colored pencils and draw in it too. Your journal is just for you, so be yourself!

When Katie got home, her dad was playing the piano. "Tell me a secret!" she said.

"I love you," said her dad.

Katie laughed and said, "I already knew that!"

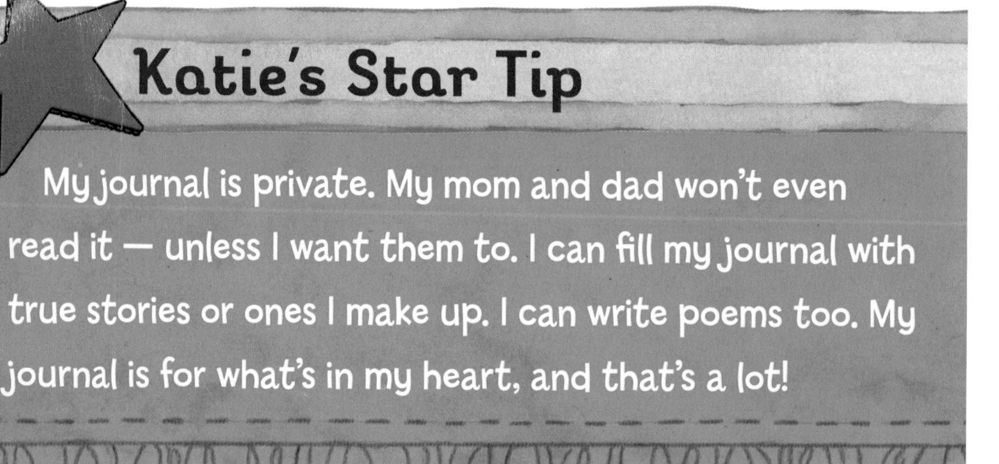

Katie's Star Tip

My journal is private. My mom and dad won't even read it — unless I want them to. I can fill my journal with true stories or ones I make up. I can write poems too. My journal is for what's in my heart, and that's a lot!

Katie asked her mom, "Did you have any secrets when you were a little girl?"

"I did," said her mom. "I was afraid to sleep on the top bunk."

"You were?" said Katie. "I'm not scared of my bunk bed."

She went into her room and climbed to the top.

And what was on the pillow? Her lucky charm!

Katie called up JoJo. “Guess what?” she said. “I found my lucky charm, but I was lucky all day without it!”

“You always are!” said JoJo. “Good night! Sleep tight.”

Katie put her journal under her pillow.

"Maybe I will write my dreams in it tomorrow," said Katie.

And she did!

Journal Writing Prompts!

A writing prompt is a question that gives you an idea for writing. Here are some fun prompts for writing in your journal:

- ✿ If you had a restaurant, what kind of food would you serve? What would the name of your restaurant be?
- ✿ Think of a time you played with an animal. What did you do? How did you feel?
- ✿ What is the best book you have ever read? Why did you like it?
- ✿ What is your favorite room in your home? What do you like to do there?

Glossary

goals—things that a person wants and tries to get or become

journal—a written record of thoughts, feelings, and experiences

journal entry—something written down in a journal

memories—people, things, or events that are remembered

private—not meant to be shared with others

prompt—something that gets you started

Read More

Loewen, Nancy. *It's All About You: Writing Your Own Journal.* Writer's Toolbox. Mankato, Minn.: Picture Window Books, 2010.

Minden, Cecilia and Kate Roth. *How to Write a Journal.* Language Arts Explorer Junior. Ann Arbor, Mich.: Cherry Lake Pub., 2011.

Pennypacker, Sara. *Clementine All About You Journal.* New York: Hyperion Books for Children, 2012.

On the Internet

- Learn more about Katie and her friends.
- Find a Katie Woo color sheet, scrapbook, and stationery.
- Discover more Katie Woo books.

All at ... www.capstonekids.com

Still Want More?

Find cool websites related to this book at *www.facthound.com.*

Just type in this code: **9781404881273** and you're ready to go!

About the Author

Fran Manushkin is the author of many popular picture books, including *Baby, Come Out!*; *Latkes and Applesauce: A Hanukkah Story*; *The Tushy Book*; *The Belly Book*; and *Big Girl Panties*. There is a real Katie Woo—she's Fran's great-niece—but she never gets in half the trouble of the Katie Woo in the books. Fran writes on her beloved Mac computer in New York City, without the help of her two naughty cats, Chaim and Goldy.

About the Illustrator

Tammie Lyon began her love for drawing at a young age while sitting at the kitchen table with her dad. She continued her love of art and eventually attended the Columbus College of Art and Design, where she earned a bachelors degree in fine art. Today she lives with her husband, Lee, in Cincinnati, Ohio. Her dogs, Gus and Dudley, keep her company as she works in her studio.

Look for all the books in the series: